AF583075

For my little horses

THE TALE OF THE HEARTBROKEN HORSE

By Alesha Harper

The heartbroken horse was so heartbroken.

He just could not write the letter Hh.

Mommy horse would say,

“HHH… hhh… hat.

Two number ones and connect them.”

But it would come out like this...

The heartbroken horse was so heartbroken.

He just could not write the letter Hh.

Mommy horse would say, "HHH... hhh... ham. Two number ones and connect them."

It still came out like this...

The heartbroken horse was so heartbroken. He just could not write the letter Hh.

Mommy horse would say,

“HHH... hhh...

hot.

Two number ones and connect them.”

But it came
out like this again.

The heartbroken horse was so heartbroken... He just could not

write the letter Hh.

Mommy horse said "I know you can do it, just breath and relax. HHH...hhh... Horse... Two number ones and connect them."

The heartbroken horse took a deep breath and said, "I know I can do it.

HHH... hhh... Horse."

Now can you guess what happened?

He made a perfect Hh!

The heartbroken horse was not heartbroken anymore!

You can do anything you put your mind to.

“Learn from yesterday, live for today, hope for tomorrow.”

{Albert Einstein}

Now you try!

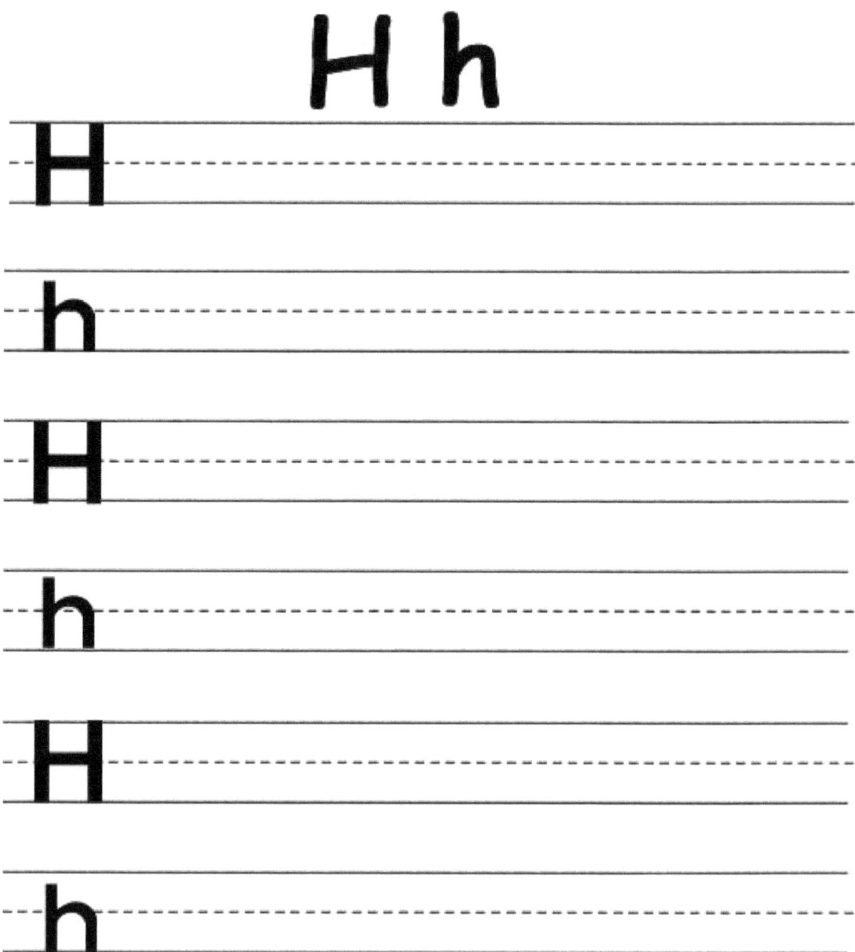

You did great!

Now you try!

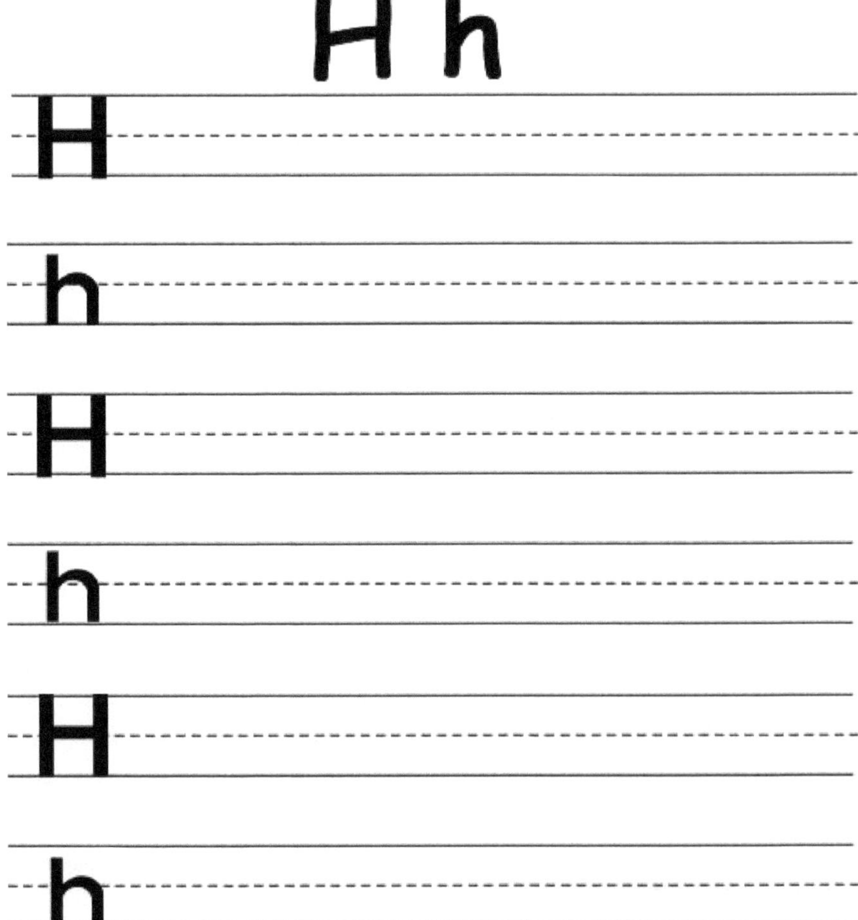

You did great!

Now you try!

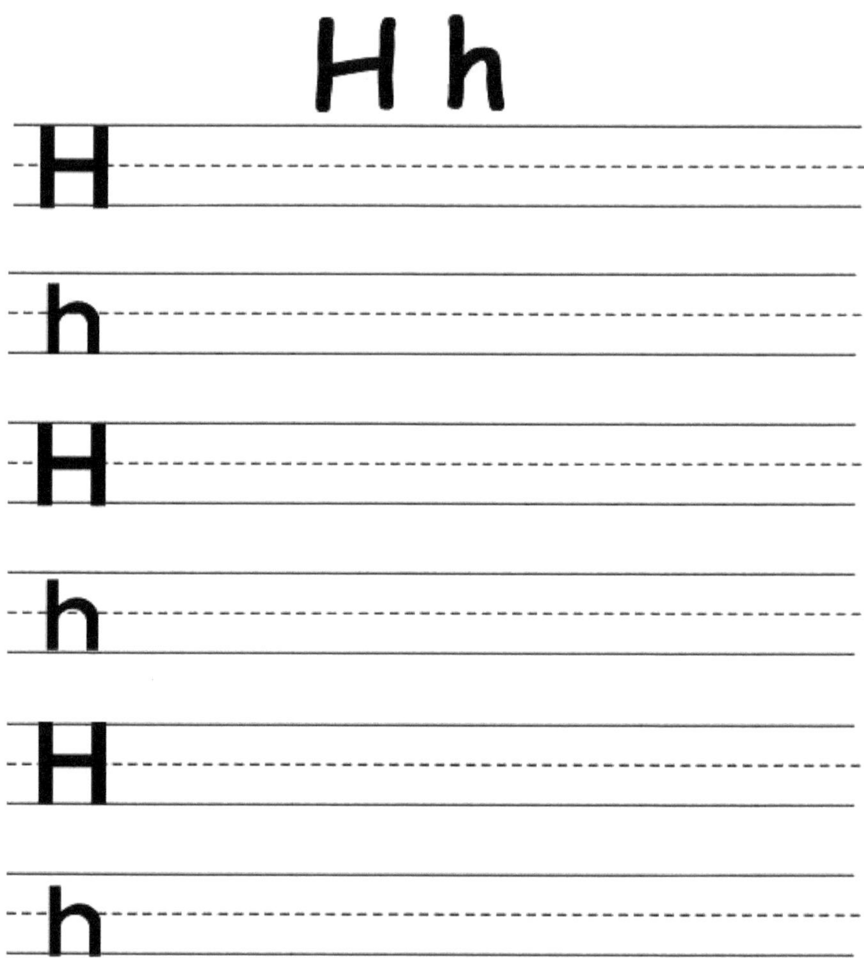

You did great!

Now you try!

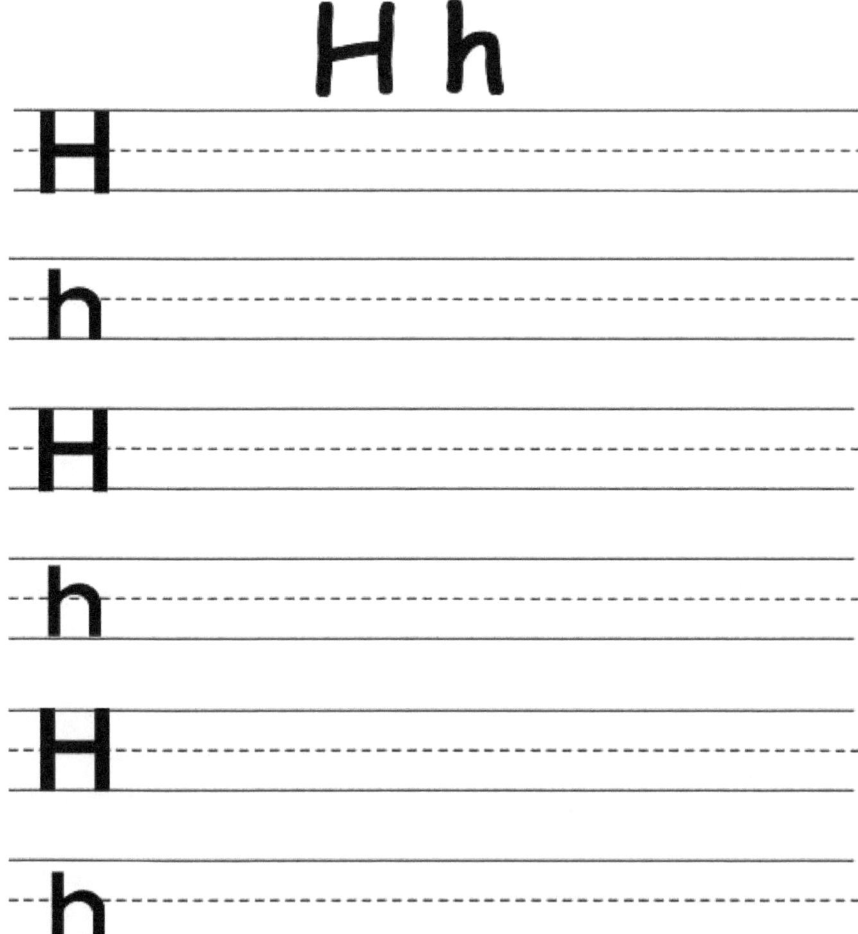

You did great!

Now you try!

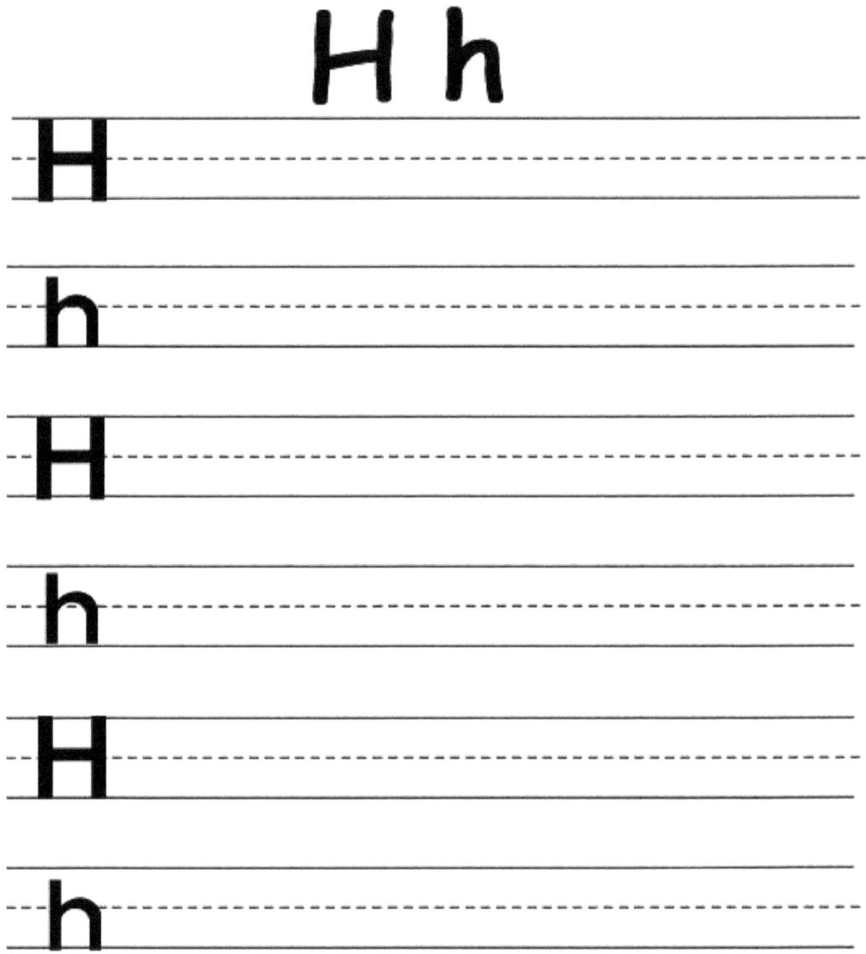

You did great!

www.ingramcontent.com/pod-product-compliance
Lightning Source LLC
LaVergne TN
LVHW021326160826
845679LV00001B/495
* 9 7 9 8 3 7 3 8 8 3 3 4 4 *